Explore Ancient India

Candice Ransom

Lerner Publications ◆ Minneapolis

Lerner Publications Company
An imprint of Lerner Publishing Group, Inc.
241 First Avenue North
Minneapolis, MN 55401 USA

For reading levels and more information, look up this title at www.lernerbooks.com.

Main body text set in Billy Infant Regular. Typeface provided by SparkyType.

Editor: Evan Villas **Photo Editor:** Giliane Mansfeldt
Lerner team: Angel Kidd

Library of Congress Cataloging-in-Publication Data

Names: Ransom, Candice F., 1952- author
Title: Explore ancient India / Candice Ransom.
Description: Minneapolis : Lerner Publications, [2026] | Series: Lightning Bolt Books. Early civilizations | Includes bibliographical references and index. | Audience: Ages 6-9 | Audience: Grades 2-3 | Summary: "Ancient India is one of the world's oldest civilizations. Its history stretches back thousands of years! Readers will discover the diverse peoples and cultures of this region and learn about their daily lives"— Provided by publisher.
Identifiers: LCCN 2025015200 (print) | LCCN 2025015201 (ebook) | ISBN 9798765689325 lib. bdg. | ISBN 9798348029012 pbk | ISBN 9798765696989 epub
Subjects: LCSH: India—Civilization—To 1200 | India—Antiquities
Classification: LCC DS425 .R335 2026 (print) | LCC DS425 (ebook) | DDC 954.02—dc23/eng/20250527

LC record available at https://lccn.loc.gov/2025015200
LC ebook record available at https://lccn.loc.gov/2025015201

Manufactured in the United States of America
1-1012509-54800-8/4/2025

Table of Contents

Moving to India

India is one of the oldest civilizations in the world. It may have begun eight thousand years ago.

India is part of the continent of Asia. India is bordered by the Indian Ocean to the south and the Himalayan mountains to the north.

Thousands of years ago, people moved into the Indus Valley, near the Indus River. They created a new civilization. It was the first in India.

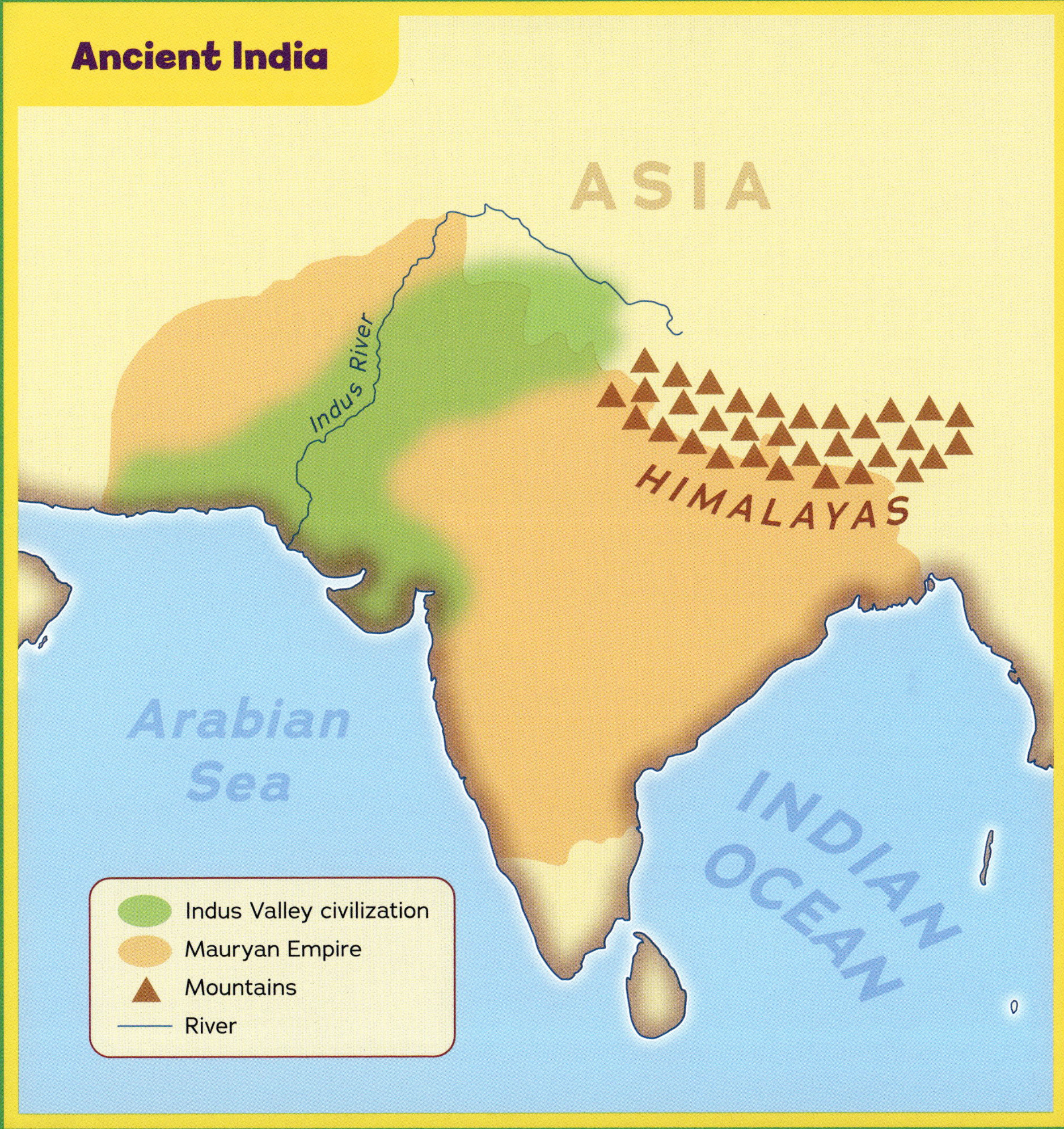
Ancient India
ASIA
Indus River
HIMALAYAS
Arabian Sea
INDIAN OCEAN
Indus Valley civilization
Mauryan Empire
Mountains
River

Civilization to Empire

The Indus Valley is in northern India. People farmed the fertile land near the Indus River.

They grew wheat, barley, peas, and other vegetables. They grew cotton and raised cattle. Dogs, cats, and Asian elephants worked on farms.

Elephants can carry heavy objects.

The people of the Indus Valley lived in cities and towns. They crafted clay toys and metal tools to trade. **They left writing that people today cannot read.**

The language of ancient India is a mystery.

Floods may have caused people to leave the valley. Their civilization ended around thirty-seven hundred years ago.

About two hundred years after that, new people came to India from central Asia. They brought a religion called Hinduism. It is thought to be the oldest religion in the world.

A statue of a Hindu god

These people also brought a new type of social system. Under this system, people were divided into four groups. Everyone had a different role.

Teachers and priests were in the highest group. Next came rulers, then traders and farmers. Last were people who did jobs most people did not want.

Around twenty-three hundred years ago, a new empire rose to power in India. It was known as the Mauryan Empire. It covered all of India except for the southern tip.

People can still visit some buildings from ancient India.

Emperor Ashoka formed a large army to keep out invaders. He also spread a religion called Buddhism.

The Fall of Ancient India

The Mauryan Empire ended twenty-two hundred years ago because of weak leaders. Five hundred years later, the Gupta Empire rose to power. Its people were great scientists, writers, and artists.

But groups from central Asia attacked the region again and again. The Gupta Empire fell and broke into smaller kingdoms fifteen hundred years ago.

People in India waiting to vote in 2025

Today, India is a democracy. **The people there choose their leaders by voting.**

A Look at Ancient India's Genius

Aryabhata was born during the Gupta Empire. He studied math and the stars. He figured out how eclipses of the sun and moon work. Midnight, he said, was the start of a new day. Aryabhata also invented the number system we still use.

Ancient India Facts

- Some experts believe the game of chess was invented in India.
- Ancient Indians used shampoo.
- Yoga was invented in India five thousand years ago.
- Cities in the Indus Valley civilization had toilets and sewer systems.

Glossary

civilization: a large group of people who share a government and culture

continent: one of the seven large landmasses on Earth

emperor: the leader of an empire

empire: a group of nations or peoples under one ruler or government

fertile: easy to grow food on

priest: a religious leader

religion: a set of beliefs about how the universe was made and what its purpose is

Learn More

Bilan, Jasbinder. *My Incredible India*. Candlewick, 2023.

Britannica Kids: Ancient India
https://kids.britannica.com/students/article/ancient-India/627684

History for Kids: Ancient India Facts for Kids
https://historyforkids.org/ancient-india/

Kiddle: Ancient India Facts for Kids
https://kids.kiddle.co/Ancient_India

Lynch, Seth. *Ancient India*. Enslow, 2025.

Wagner, Zelda. *Explore Ancient Egypt*. Lerner Publications, 2026.

Index

Photo Acknowledgments

Image credits: Ayse Topbas/Getty Images, p. 4; Jenner Images/Getty Images, p. 5; anand purohit/Getty Images, p. 6; Sajjad Maqsood/Getty Images, p. 7; Laura Westlund/Independent Picture Service, p. 8; chuchart duangdaw/Getty Images, p. 9; De Agostini/Getty Images, p. 10; DEA PICTURE LIBRARY/De Agostini/Getty Images, p. 11; RBB/Getty Images, p. 12; Zaporizhzhia vector/Shutterstock, p. 13; Corbis/VCG/Getty Images, p. 14; Pallava Bagla/Corbis/Getty Images, p. 15; Fine Art Images/Heritage Images/Getty Images, p. 16; CMA/BOT/Alamy, p. 17; Hans Neleman/Getty Images, p. 18; Anuwar Hazarika/NurPhoto/Getty Images, p. 19; Dinodia Photos/Alamy, p. 20.

Cover: CRS PHOTO/Shutterstock.